GERMANY

UNPACKED

Clive Gifford

WAYLAND
www.waylandbooks.co.uk

Published in paperback in 2017 by Wayland
Copyright © Hodder and Stoughton, 2017

Editor: Nicola Edwards
Designer: Peter Clayman
Cover design: Matthew Kelly

Dewey number: 943'.0883–dc23
ISBN: 978 0 7502 9168 2
10 9 8 7 6 5 4 3 2 1

MIX
Paper from
responsible sources
FSC
www.fsc.org
FSC® C104740

Wayland, an imprint of
Hachette Children's Group
Part of Hodder and Stoughton
Carmelite House
50 Victoria Embankment
London EC4Y 0DZ

An Hachette UK Company
www.hachette.co.uk
www.hachettechildrens.co.uk

Printed and bound in China

Picture acknowledgements: All images and graphic elements courtesy of Shutterstock except
p5 (br), p21 (b) and p27 (t) Corbis.com.

Contents

Germany: Unpacked

UNPACKED

Welcome to Germany! You've arrived in one of Europe's largest and most populous countries, packed with forests and rivers, sprawling cities and a complex, fascinating history. Germany is an economic powerhouse and home to some of the world's biggest companies. Did you know that jet aircraft and X-rays were first developed in Germany or that German pioneers invented the automobile and the aspirin? To learn about Germany's castles, cars and culture, its spectacular cities and some of its most famous citizens, just keep on reading!

Fact File

Area: 357,168 sq km
Population: 82 million (2014 est.)
Capital city: Berlin
Land borders: Austria, Belgium, Czech Republic, Denmark, France, Luxembourg, Netherlands, Poland, Switzerland
Currency: The Euro

Flag:

Symbols: Germany's national tree is the oak and its coat of arms features a black eagle.

Germany

You can see from this map how Germany is bordered by nine countries. Germany's capital, Berlin, is shown too, along with some of the other places you can read about in this book.

North Sea

Denmark

Baltic Sea

Hamburg

Elbe

BERLIN

Poland

Netherlands

Rhine

Leipzig

Oder

Dusseldorf

Dresden

Cologne

Germany

Belgium

Main

Czech Republic

Luxembourg

Stuttgart

Danube

France

Munich

Zugspitze
(highest point)

Switzerland

Austria

Berlin, Germany's largest city has an area of 892 square kilometres – nine times bigger than Paris. It also has more than 1,700 bridges.

Spreuerhofstrasse, the world's narrowest street, is in Reutlingen, southern Germany, and is just 31 cm wide at its narrowest point.

Forests, Rivers and Lakes

Germany consists of three broad regions. There are the northern plains, which border the North and Baltic Seas and give Germany its 2,390km of coastline, a central region, and the southern uplands, including the country's highest point, the 2,693m tall peak of Zugspitze, on the border with Austria.

Wood You Believe It?

Germany is home to beavers and wild boar amongst other creatures that make their homes in and around the woodlands of the country. Germany is one of the most wooded nations in Europe, with over 30 per cent of its land covered in forests of fir, pine, beech, oak and birch. The Bavarian Forest in the south is the largest mountain forest in Europe, while the scenic Black Forest region attracts millions of visitors each year.

Germany has around 2.5 million timber-framed houses – more than any other country in Europe.

The River Elbe flows through the city of Dresden in eastern Germany.

Water Courses

Germany has many rivers, a dozen of which are over 180 km long, including parts of the two longest rivers of Europe, the Rhine and the Danube. Approximately 865 km of the mighty Rhine flows through the country providing, along with other rivers including the 700km-long Elbe, important waterways for cargo as well as travel and leisure. A giant, 171km canal built between the Danube and Main rivers has helped connect waterways so that it is possible to carry cargo from the North Sea all the way to the Black Sea.

Lakes and Caves

Germany has over 1,000 lakes in one region alone – the Mecklenburg Lakeland region. The country's largest lake is Lake Constance, which it shares with Switzerland, and many of its lakes are used for fishing, canoeing and windsurfing. Much of Germany's land lies on limestone rock, which has been eroded over time to form many cave systems. Germany has more than 50 'show caves' on view to the public, including Devil's Cave, which is over 1,500m long, and Bear's Cave, so named for the skeletons of now extinct cave bears found there.

In the Falkensteiner cave lurks a crocodile - a metre-long stalactite that has fallen from the ceiling.

East And West

Germany was for many centuries a collection of many individual cities and states, large and small, which ruled themselves. In 1871, they were united as a single nation and ruled by an emperor, but in the 20th Century after World War II the country was divided again.

Split Up

After Germany's defeat in 1945, the country was divided into four zones, each occupied by a different Allied force. Four years later, the eastern zone under the control of the Soviet Union became a separate nation, the German Democratic Republic (DDR), while the western parts occupied by France, Britain and the USA became the Federal Republic of Germany (FRG). For more than four decades, East and West Germany were separate nations with different political systems, economies and different nations as their allies.

The Berlin Wall

Germany's former capital city, Berlin, remained divided for the next 40 years, even more so after East Germany constructed a heavily armed 43km concrete wall in 1961 to stop its citizens defecting to West Germany. The wall became a symbol of the divided city and nation.

Parts of the Berlin Wall remain standing today, covered in graffiti.

City of Spies

The period from the end of the World War II to the start of the 1990s is known as the Cold War. It was a period of tension and hostility between the USA and the Soviet Union and their respective allies, with East and West Germany right on the frontline. As a divided city, Berlin was packed full of spies trying to learn the other side's secrets. Sometimes, captured spies were exchanged by both sides at Berlin's Glienicke Bridge.

Glienicke Bridge spans the Havel River.

Together Again

In 1989, the Berlin Wall was torn down amidst wild celebrations. The following year, German reunification saw the country became whole again, with Helmut Kohl elected the country's chancellor and leader. Germany is now divided into 13 regions and 3 city areas, all known as Länder, with Berlin again the country's capital. In 2005, Germany elected its first female chancellor, Angela Merkel.

The 3rd of October is a national holiday, with fireworks at Berlin's Brandenburg Gate celebrating reunification.

Dinner Time!

German cuisine is not all sausages and sauerkraut (pickled cabbage), although sausages, known as *Wurst*, are pretty important! Germans eat more than 300 different types of bread and there are dozens of different dishes throughout each region of the country.

Best and Wurst

There are an estimated 1,500 different types of sausage available in Germany. Munich, for example, has its very own white sausage, called *Weisswurst*, which is only served before noon. In some restaurants, sausages are served with a dish called *himmel und erde* (meaning heaven and earth), which is mashed potatoes and apples. One of the most popular sausage snacks of all is the spicy currywurst, mostly bought from street vendors. A staggering 800 million were sold in 2013, vying with donor kebabs as German's favourite takeout treat. There's even a museum in Berlin dedicated to the currywurst!

Regional Recipes

Every region of Germany has its own specialites. These include roasted pork knuckle in Bavaria, stewed eels along Germany's northern coast, dumplings in parts of northern Germany and beetroot soup, which is often eaten in eastern Germany. Not for the weak of stomach, *Schwarzsauer* is a German stew made of goose giblets, blood, vinegar and peppercorns, while in the central German village of Würchwitz, *Milbenkäse* cheese is made containing 0.5-0.7mm-long living cheese mites. Urgh!

A stewed eel dish from northern Germany.

Weisswurst is usually eaten with sweet mustard and a pretzel.

Bavarian pork knuckle on a bed of sauerkraut.

A Sweet Tooth

For all their savoury delights, many Germans have a sweet tooth, including Hans Riegel who in 1922 invented the gummy bear that helped build the Haribo empire. Popular sweet treats include apple strudel, a light pastry filled with apples and raisins flavoured with cinnamon, and stollen – cakes made with marzipan and dried fruit.

Stollen cake is celebrated every year at a festival in Dresden.

Beer's Here

Germany is home to over 1,200 breweries, far more than any other European nation. Four of these are located in the small German settlement of Aufsess, which has just 1,500 inhabitants. Around 5,000 different beers are produced and enjoyed at many different beer festivals. Biggest of all is the Oktoberfest in Munich, which first took place in 1810 and is still going today. More than six million visitors come to enjoy the beer, food, music and entertainment at each annual 16-day Oktoberfest at which almost 7 million litres of beer are served.

Revellers enjoy Oktoberfest inside a giant beer tent.

NO WAY!

The lost property office at the Oktoberfest is kept busy. In 2013, amongst the lost items were hundreds of mobile phones and passports, two wedding rings, A Bayern Munich garden gnome and one set of false teeth!

Energy and Ecology

As a major industrial nation, one of the biggest in the world, Germany needs large amounts of power. It gets its electricity mostly from coal-fuelled power stations, but renewable 'green' energy use is increasing.

NO WAY!

There are more than 1.4 million solar power systems installed in Germany, many on the rooftops of houses.

The Bagger 293 can remove up to 240,000m³ from the ground every day.

Mine Time

Germany has reserves of minerals like rocksalt and potash, which are used in its chemicals industry, but its biggest mines are for coal, particularly in the Ruhr region of the country and for lower grade brown coal in eastern Germany. At these latter mines, giant machines called bucket wheel excavators carve out the ground. The Bagger 293 at work near Hambach is one of the world's biggest. It is 225m long and weighs 13,500 tonnes.

Renewable Energy

As much as a fifth of Germany's electricity has been generated using nuclear power, but the country plans to phase this out by the 2020s, instead using more and more renewable energy sources, such as hydroelectric, solar and wind power. Around one in five of all the world's advanced solar cells (which convert sunlight to electricity) are produced in Germany, while the country also has more than 21,000 wind turbines which help generate about 8 per cent of all its electricity.

Solar panels on the houses in a 'solar village' in Freiburg.

⬆ People gather at a demonstration in Munich to protest against nuclear power.

The Green Movement

The word 'ecology' was invented by the German naturalist Ernst Haeckel in 1869, and many Germans have been at the forefront of movements to protect the planet. Germany was one of the first countries to have a Green Party, and today the Green Parliamentary Group has more than 60 members in the Bundestag, the German parliament. Germans recycle more than 60 per cent of all municipal waste – one and a half times the rate of the UK.

Knights and Castles

The area that is now known as Germany was for many centuries, from the Middle Ages onwards, a large number of small states, kingdoms and independent cities. These all jostled for territory and power and frequently fought each other.

Kriebstein Castle looms over the River Zschopau.

Scenic Strongholds

Nobles secured their territory against threats from all directions, often by building forts or castles, some of which survive to this day. Many, such as Kriebstein Castle, were placed on high cliffs overlooking rivers or, like Heidelberg Castle, on steep hill slopes to give commanding views of the town and surrounding areas below. Built to protect the Dukes of Bavaria and their gold and silver, Burghausen Castle is a mighty fortress with five courtyards, massive stone walls and has a length of 1,004 m, making it the longest castle complex in Europe.

A German stamp commemorates the life of Gottfried von Berlichingen.

Mighty Knights

Knights rode on horseback, wore heavy armour and wielded maces, spears and lethal swords in battle. Many were mercenaries, fighting for whichever kingdom or territory would pay them. Few German knights are more celebrated than Gottfried von Berlichingen. He lost his right arm during the siege of the city of Landshut in 1504 when a cannon shot forced his own sword through his arm. Wearing a replacement mechanical hand and arm made of iron, he battled on for a further 40 years through dozens of campaigns before retiring to Hornburg Castle.

NO WAY!

Neuschwanstein castle featured over 400 tonnes of marble for its window frames alone, which all had to be transported from Austria by hand.

Forts and Fantasies

By the 19th Century, the knights had long gone, but that did not stop some wealthy German nobles building their own fairy-tale castles that harked back to a different age. Ludwig II, King of Bavaria, ordered the building of the majestic, 150m-long, Neuschwanstein Castle in 1869. It was complete with an indoor waterfall, two of Europe's first ever telephones and woodwork so intricate that it took 14 carpenters over four years to complete one room!

Neuschwanstein Castle attracts over 1.3 million visitors per year.

Football Crazy!

A lthough Germans love motorsports, basketball, ice hockey, handball and cycling, football is far and away Germany's number one sport. Almost one in ten of the entire population are registered as football players and there are more than 26,000 football clubs in the country.

NO WAY!

The world's best goalkeeper, Germany's Manuel Neuer, is also a top quizzer. He won half a million Euros on the German edition of the TV quiz show, *Who Wants To Be A Millionaire?*

Bouncing Bundesliga

The top German clubs ply their trade in the Bundesliga, an 18-team league, which first began in 1963. The Bundesliga is the best supported football league in the world with an average attendance of over 45,000 for every single game of the season. Bayern Munich are its most successful side, winning the league a record 24 times including back-to-back successes in 2014 and 2015.

Football fans are passionate in support of their teams at Germany's Bundesliga matches.

Fan-Tastic

Football is followed with fervour and passion in Germany. The biggest clubs are not allowed to be owned by one rich owner. Instead, they each have thousands of members. Tickets to see top sides like Bayern Munich and Borussia Dortmund can be as little as a quarter of the price of an English Premier League match, and many grounds have standing sections. The most magnificent of all is the Yellow Wall, a stand running the entire length of the pitch at Borussia Dortmund's Signal Iduna Park stadium, which can hold 25,000 noisy supporters, all wearing the yellow and black colours of their club.

World Champions

On the international stage, Germany are always one of the favourites come competition time and with good reason. They have won the FIFA World Cup four times, been runners-up a further four times and hosted the World Cup three times (in 1954, 1974 and 1990). They have scored more goals than any other team at the last three World Cups. Germany's veteran striker, Miroslav Klose, is the World Cup's all-time leading scorer with 16 goals to his name. The German women's team is equally successful, having won the Women's World Cup twice (in 2003 and 2007) and a record six European Championships in a row.

It's easy to see how the Yellow Wall stand got its name!

Miroslav Klose celebrates another goal.

Super Cities

Germany is packed with medium-sized towns and smaller cities — more than one thousand of them. But only four cities have a population of over one million: Berlin — the country's capital — and the cities of Cologne, Hamburg and Munich.

Cologne is a popular destination for tourists and hosts a carnival every year in the spring.

Cool Cologne

Founded as an outpost of the Roman empire almost 2,000 years ago, Cologne lies beside the Rhine and was one of the biggest and most wealthy trading centres in medieval Europe. Visitors today are drawn to the 12 Romanesque churches within its medieval city walls, the appetising-sounding Chocolate Museum and the giant cathedral which took an incredible 632 years to complete (1248-1880). They also come for more than 50 large trade fairs held throughout the year and flock to the Cologne Carnival, one of the biggest street fairs in Europe.

A Phenomenal Port

Hamburg is Germany's second largest city. It is also the biggest port in the country and the second biggest in Europe. Located on the River Elbe, more than 10,000 ships each year sail in and out, carrying over 130 million tonnes of goods and materials and linking with some 6,000 freight trains every month. The city grew wealthy from its sea trade from the Middle Ages onwards. It boasts a lavish town hall with 647 rooms, giant art galleries and a large number of canals crossed by more than 2,400 bridges.

You'll need to climb 436 steps to reach the top of Hamburg Town Hall's 112m-high tower.

NO WAY!

The flowing waters of the Eisbach River form a 1m-tall standing wave, allowing people to surf in the middle of Munich!

Marvellous Munich

Munich's name means 'Home of the Monks' and it started out as a monastery. Later it was ruled by one family, the Wittelsbachs, for more than 700 years. Located in the south-east of Germany and a gateway to the Alps mountain range, it is a city of culture with over 60 theatres, 40 museums and more than 200 publishing houses. Many of its main city streets were pedestrianized for the 1972 Olympic Games and have remained free of cars ever since. Munich's giant city park is full of Asian pagodas and influences but is named the Englischer Garten (English Garden) and parts of it are used by nudists!

Surfing in Munich on the 2km-long Eisbach River.

Big Brains

German innovation and new thinking in the sciences and philosophy has resulted in a whole hatful of breakthroughs over the years. Particularly brainy Germans have notched up 20 Nobel Prizes for Physics, including the very first, awarded to Wilhelm Conrad Röntgen in 1901 for his discovery of X-rays.

NO WAY!

Madcap inventor Dieter Michael Krone built the Papierflieger-Maschinenpistole – a machine gun that folds paper to create paper planes, which it shoots out of its barrel!

Extraordinary Engineers

Germany's enterprising engineers built the first jet engine aircraft, the Heinkel He 178, giant passenger-carrying airships and invented diesel engines as well as the electron microscope. Werner von Braun pioneered the first long-range rocket missile, the V2, and later led American efforts into space, building the *Saturn V* Moon rocket. German computer pioneers include Konrad Zuse, who built the first electronic computers in the late 1930s onwards, and scientists at the Fraunhofer Institute who invented the MP3 file for digital sound.

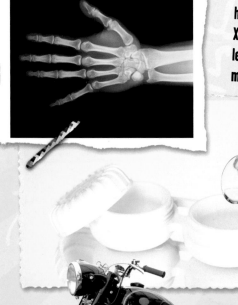

German inventors have given us X-rays, contact lenses and the motorbike!

Big Thinkers

This statue of Marx (left) and Engels is found near Alexanderplatz in Berlin.

Many German philosophers, from Frederik Nietzsche to Immanuel Kant, have studied why people are like they are, ways they can live together and how they interact with others and the world around them. Some, such as Hannah Arendt and Karl Marx, have influenced politics with their works. Marx and his fellow-German, Friedrich Engels, co-wrote *The Communist Manifesto* in 1845 and Marx also wrote *Das Kapital*.

Awesome Albert

Born in Ulm in 1879 and schooled in Munich, Albert Einstein became the world's most famous scientist for his work on space, time and gravity and showing how energy and matter are related with the famous equation, $E=MC^2$. He won a Nobel Prize in 1921 for his work on the photoelectric effect and investigated light in ways that helped later scientists build lasers. Einstein was a quirky character who hated wearing socks, never learned to drive and in 1952 was asked if he would become President of Israel! He politely declined.

Brilliant scientist Albert Einstein at work.

Great Days Out

G ermany has a wealth of things for visitors to do. It boasts more museums and galleries than any other nation in Europe - a whopping 6,300 or so dotted all over the country. Some, like the Neues Museum in Berlin and the Zwinger in Dresden (right), are world renowned. Others, like the Museum of Snoring in Alfeld, are rather less well known!

Miniature Wonderland's model railway includes 890 trains with more than 11,000 carriages.

Mad Museums

Amongst Germany's many museums are some decidedly odd collections. Titisee is home to the Cuckoo Clock Museum, while Dusseldorf has the Senfmuseum devoted just to mustard. There's also an entire museum in Munich dedicated to potato art. The world's largest model railway can be found at Miniature Wonderland in Hamburg, complete with 15,000m of track.

Zoos with a View

Germany has a long history of enjoying exotic animals ever since Charlemagne received an elephant from an Arab emperor and brought it back to Augsberg more than 1,200 years ago. Leipzig Zoo has bred more than 2,000 lions and 250 rare Siberian tigers and also possesses the largest tropical house in Europe. Inside this centrally-heated building, which is bigger than two football pitches, live more than 100 tropical species, including tapirs and pygmy hippos. Berlin Zoo is Germany's oldest surviving zoo, having opened in 1844. It is also the biggest with over 20,000 animals gazed at by more than three million visitors every year.

Berlin Zoo is home to more than 1,500 species, including these Emperor penguins.

Park Life

Germany's oldest surviving nature reserve was established at Lüneburg Heath in 1921. It has since been joined by more than 3,000 similarly protected areas, including 15 large national parks in which many Germans enjoy hiking, cycling or canoeing. There are wildcats in the beech forests of the Eifel National Park near Germany's border with Belgium, while the Eurasian lynx, peregrine falcons and black storks are found in the Harz National Park.

Brown bears roam parts of the Bayerischer Wald National Park.

The Car's the Star

Germany is the birthplace of the motor industry. In 1885, Karl Benz produced his Patent Motorwagen. This three-wheeler was the first car powered by an internal combustion engine. Daimler followed with the first four-wheeled car a year later and Germany was also the home of the first production motorcycles.

NO WAY!

The one millionth VW Beetle to be produced was sprayed in gold and had its bumpers covered in rhinestones!

Major Motors

Germany produces 5.9 million cars a year – more than any other European nation. In addition, a further 5.5 million German branded cars are produced overseas. Leading manufacturers include Audi, Porsche, Mercedes and BMW. Volkswagen is the biggest of all and nearly two million visitors flock to its Wolfsburg headquarters each year to see the Autostadt museum there and to collect their newly-built cars from two giant towers, each holding 400 vehicles. Each car in the tower is parked by robot – a process that takes less than two minutes.

 BMW's headquarters in Munich are shaped like an engine with four cylinders!

Germany is the world's fourth-largest producer of new cars, after Japan, the USA and China.

Beetling About

Of all the many car models produced in Germany, the VW Beetle (below) remains the most famous. First constructed in the 1930s as an affordable 'people's car', early Beetles were very basic – but that didn't stop the orders flooding in. By the time production of the cars ended in 2003, a record 21.5 million had been produced.

On the Road

Germany has a staggering 650,000km of roads, almost twice as many as in the UK. Some 13,000km of these are famous high speed roads called autobahns. The first, between Cologne and Bonn, opened in 1932. The autobahns originally had no speed limit, allowing a Mercedes W125 Rekordwagen to rocket along at 432km/h – over three and a half times the UK speed limit! Today, top speeds are recommended and enforced for some types of vehicle such as buses, but many autobahns still offer seriously high-speed driving.

Stars in Cars

Motorsport attracts huge interest in Germany which has its own touring car championships, the Deutsche Tourenwagen Masters, amongst many domestic race competitions. On the Formula One circuit, German drivers hold a number of records, including the youngest ever world champion, Sebastien Vettel, and the most successful driver of all, Michael Schumacher, with 91 race wins and seven World Championship triumphs.

Sebastien Vettel had achieved 70 top-three finishes in Grand Prix racing by the time he was 27 years old.

Quirky Germany

Germany can be a funny place. When Germans tell the time and say, 'half past six', they actually mean 'half an hour before six' – 5.30! Germans also invented the game of underwater rugby, while Munich hosted the first Extreme Ironing World Championships in 2002. Here's plenty more oddities and quirks of this fascinating country.

Love and Marriage

Germans have some decidedly odd traditions concerning romance. Couples in Cologne, for example, fix padlocks, known as 'love locks' to the railings of Hohenzollern Bridge and then, to ensure everlasting love, throw the key away into the river. If love turns to marriage, then couples may have to endure a pair of peculiar procedures. In some parts of rural Germany, the bride-to-be is kidnapped during the wedding reception and the groom has to find her. Another tradition is *Polterabend*. It's a dinner party held by the bride and groom before the wedding in which guests smash the plates for luck and leave the soon-to-be newlyweds to clear up all the mess.

Thousands of padlocks greet people crossing the Rhine on Hohenzollern Bridge.

Strange Days Out

Amongst Germany's many visitor attractions is the weird Wunderland Kalkar. This theme park is built on the site of an old nuclear power station whose giant cooling tower has been turned into a climbing wall on the outside while a fairground ride operates on the inside. For winter sports fans, the AlpinCenter in Bottrop is Europe's longest indoor ski slope, all 640m of its snowy length. Summer holidays can be taken all-year-round in the Tropical Island Resort, a giant dome heated to a constant 26°C which contains a 140m-long pool, acting as the sea and a 200m-long indoor beach – the longest in the world.

Around 600,000 people visit Wunderland Kalkar and its rides every year.

NO WAY!

A tradition for millions of Germans on New Year's Eve is to stay in and watch a British TV comedy from the 1960s called *Dinner For One.*

This star tells visitors that they've reached the Zugspitze, the highest point in Germany.

Leisure with Laughs

Travellers with a taste for the unusual can sleep in a beer barrel at Ostbever's Landhotel Beverland or spend the night in an igloo made of snow at the top of Zugspitze – the country's highest point. In October they could visit Stuttgart to watch the Tübingen Duck Race involving 7,000 bright yellow rubber ducks racing along the river. It's quackers!

All the Arts

Germany and its people have made a major impact on the arts, from Johann Gutenberg, the first European to print books using movable type, to the Berlin International Film Festival, where leading movies compete for the honour of winning the festival's Golden and Silver Bear awards.

NO WAY!

JS Bach had 20 children, four of whom went on to be classical composers in their own right.

Tellers of Tales

Germans are avid readers and the country has been home to many fine wordsmiths, from playwrights such as Bertolt Brecht to Gunter Grass, one of Germany's 13 winners of the Nobel Prize for Literature. Born in Hanau, Jacob and Wilhelm Grimm were language scholars who scoured Germany to collect traditional folk tales and write them down to record them for history. The pair gathered dozens of stories, which were first published in 1812 then rewritten and added to many times throughout the 19th Century. Some of the tales told by the Brothers Grimm have become world-famous, such as Hansel and Gretel, Little Red Riding Hood, Snow White and Rapunzel.

A bronze sculpture of the Bremen Town Musicians – characters in one of the Brothers Grimm's tales.

Visitors admire an exhibition of modern art in Berlin including paintings by Gerhard Richter.

Painting and Sculptures

From medieval painters of religious subjects to wild and wacky abstract modern art, Germany has had it all. Famous names include Nuremberg-born Albrecht Dürer and Hans Holbein the Younger, who were both influenced by Italian renaissance art through to 20th Century painter and printmaker Otto Dix and abstract and realist painter Gerhard Richter. More than 540 pieces of Richter's art have each been sold for over £60,000. In 2015, one piece, *Abstraktes Bild*, sold for £30.4 million!

The magnificent interior of the Opera House in Dresden.

Classical to the Core

German composers from Ludwig van Beethoven and JS Bach to Richard Strauss, Joseph Hadyn and Richard Wagner have influenced classical music for centuries. Germany has 130 symphony orchestras and 80 publicly-funded concert halls as well as many large festivals in which classical works and music by modern composers, such as Karlheinz Stockhausen, are played. Germany also boasts a staggering 65,000 choirs whilst the world's longest piece of music is currently being performed on a church organ in the German town of Halberstadt. The piece, called *As Slow As Possible*, is supposed to last 639 years (that's how old the organ was in the year 2000)!

More Information

Websites

http://www.germany.travel/en/index.html
See the sights and learn about many key attractions in Germany.

http://www.germany.info/Vertretung/usa/en/04__W__t__G/05/__Kids__Teens.html
Divided into sections for kids and teens, this handy website contains interesting information on lots of topics from the Berlin Wall to snacks and music in Germany.

http://www.ukgermanconnection.org/kids-school-day
Learn more about a typical school day in Germany, picking up some German words along the way, at this great website. Do look at all the Find Out pages, which contain quizzes and amazing facts.

Apps

Wie Geht's German
Learn German with this fun and free app available on iTunes and Google Play, which has short, interactive lessons on colours, days of the week and much more besides.

Tourias Berlin Travel Guide
A simple, pictorial guide to over 100 key locations in Germany's capital city.

German States Germany Quiz
Learn about all 16 states of Germany, their location on maps and their symbols using this fun quiz available for Android devices at the Google Play store.

Movies

Missile to Moon
This PBS documentary tells the incredible story of rocket pioneer, Werner von Braun and how he helped usher in the space age.

Maya The Bee
Animated series based on the bestselling German children's book written by Waldemar Bonsels and first published in 1912.

The Miracle of Bern
A PG-rated movie about a young boy and his father and the events leading up to the 1954 World Cup which West Germany won.

Clips

https://www.youtube.com/watch?v=oO-b-D6TCpY
Check out the amazing robot car park at Volkswagen's car factories in Wolfsburg.

https://www.youtube.com/watch?v=ANttiNJ3SxY
See a gallery of views of the Tropical Island resort with its indoor beach.

https://www.youtube.com/watch?v=3COsAKsATCk
Watch a nine minute mini-documentary about the fairy-tale Neuschwanstein Castle built by Ludwig I.

Books

Discover Countries: Germany - Camilla de la Bédoyère
(Wayland, 2009)

Germany in Our World - Michael Burgan
(Franklin Watts, 2010)

Germany (Food and Celebrations) - Sylvia Goulding
(Wayland, 2008)

The first school for training guide dogs was opened in 1916 in Oldenburg in Germany, to assist soldiers who had been blinded by poisonous gas during World War I.

Glossary

Bundesliga The top league competition for football clubs in Germany.

cathedral A Christian church that is the seat or base of a bishop – a senior figure in the church.

economy The wealth, industry and resources in a country.

electron microscope An advanced microscope that uses a beam of electrons to view tiny things in detail.

eroded To have been worn away gradually over time.

giblets The liver, heart and neck of a chicken or other type of fowl.

hydroelectric power The use of the force of moving water to generate energy, usually in the form of electricity.

igloo A dome-shaped house made of compacted snow.

intricate Describes something that is highly complicated and detailed.

monk A religious man who lives alone or in a monastery with other monks.

nuclear power The splitting of atoms to generate electricity in nuclear power stations.

pedestrianized Describes a street that has been closed off to cars and other motorized traffic so that it can only be used by people on foot.

recycle To convert waste into reusable materials and goods.

reunification To reunite and make whole something that was previously split up. Germany was reunified in 1990.

tonne A unit of weight equal to 1,000kg.

Index